MW00902191

This book belongs to:

____

Copyright © 2017 Studio O

All rights reserved.